Clothed In Armor

Spiritual Warfare for Kids

Clothed In Armor
Spiritual Warfare for Kids

CLOTHED IN ARMOR
SPIRITUAL WARFARE FOR KIDS

Carol Lozier, MSW, LCSW

Praise for *Clothed in Armor*
Spiritual Warfare for Kids

"A very necessary tool for kids today. What a great talent you have!"
　　Dione Fields, RN, CCM

ALSO BY CAROL LOZIER, LCSW

The Adoptive & Foster Parent Guide: How to Heal Your Child's Trauma and Loss

Devotions of Comfort and Hope for Adoptive & Foster Moms

Clothed In Armor: Spiritual Warfare for Adopted & Foster Kids

Copyright © 2015 by Carol Lozier, LCSW

ISBN: 978-1512337099
Printed in the USA
All rights reserved

Many of the scriptures in this text were taken from the ESV (English Standard Version), NIV (New International Version), MSG (The Message), or NLT (New Living Translation) The Holy Bible, English Standard Version Copyright © 2001 by Crossway Bibles, a division of Good News Publishers.

No portion of this book may be reproduced, stored in a retrieval system or transmitted in any form or by any means—electronic, mechanical, photocopy, recording, scanning, or other-- except for brief quotations in critical reviews or articles, without the prior written permission of the author.

The information presented in this book is for informative purposes only and not intended as a medical directive. The content is not intended to be a substitute for medical or psychological advice rendered by a qualified, licensed professional. Treatment choices are at the sole discretion of the parent or individual, and should be made in consultation with a qualified psychologist, physician, or therapist. Readers are strongly encouraged to consult with their psychologist, physician, or therapist regarding any course of treatment, and assume the risk of any failure to do so. In reading this book, the reader acknowledges that the author bears no responsibility the reader's own treatment choices.

DEDICATION

As always . . . For Rachel and Aaron.

ACKNOWLEDGEMENTS

A very special thank you to the cover page artist, Reidona Shepherd. Here is a little bit about Reidi in her own words:

"Hi my name is Reidona Elise Shepherd. I am from Albania. I am adopted to a new family and have a biological sister who was adopted with me. I was nine when I got adopted, and now I am eleven…almost twelve. I love to be with my family, and I love to draw. I have three brothers, there are seven people in the family. Before I was adopted, I didn't know about God or who He was. When I was with my new family we did different things and it seemed very odd. As I got older I started to understand why we did those things and I started reading the Bible. We are all still learning, even when we are 65, and I hope you will read the Bible too."

Also, thank you to the children and parents who took their time to provide their thoughts about the study. Thank you to the following,
Susan and Tim Thieneman
Cathy Wilson
Heather Borntraeger

TABLE OF CONTENTS

Introduction	9
Week One: My Story	12
Week Two: God's Trustworthy Protection	19
Week Three: Satan is Sly	25
Week Four: Satan's Lies	31
Week Five: Fight Back!	37
Week Six: God is My Helper, My Protector	43
Appendix A	48
Appendix B	49
Appendix C	50

INTRODUCTION

Welcome to the *Clothed In Armor* Bible study! I hope and pray that this study will help your child in a new way that you hadn't even considered before today. As a Licensed Clinical Social Worker for over 25 years, (and a mom to my two precious kids) I have worked with many children and now hope to bring my knowledge to this Bible study for your child.

In the Bible study, you and your child will identify any unresolved, past hurts that Satan is currently using to create feelings of doubt, self-criticism, and hopelessness. Instead of falling prey to Satan's ploys, your child will learn how to guard him or her self with the whole armor of God. Our goal is to help your child identify and understand THE TRUTH about themselves and others, and specific ways they can fight these detrimental thoughts.

The study will also show your child that a part of their emotional struggle is the result of a spiritual battle between good (God) and evil (Satan). This understanding offers your child emotional distance from the negative beliefs instead of accepting them as truth, or as an accurate depiction of who they are as an individual.

When children have any type of hurt in their lives, they can develop and believe negative (sad or angry or critical) thoughts about themselves or others, even when the past hurtful situation is over. In the world of therapy, these hurts are often called, "traumas."

What is Trauma?

The word trauma may sound like an exaggeration to you, so let's look at it's meaning along with some examples. In a traumatic event, the child experiences a threat or assault to their emotional or physical safety or well-being and feels overwhelmed.

Trauma is identified as either one large event (large T trauma) or an ongoing series of smaller events (small t trauma). Some examples of large "T" Trauma are: natural disasters; physical, emotional or sexual abuse; neglect; serious accidents; sudden loss of a loved one; domestic violence; and small "t" trauma includes: name calling; intimidating glares; divorce; multiple moves in their school or community; physical disabilities; being teased by peers; loss of a beloved pet; an under functioning (depressed, substance addicted, absent) parent; a sibling with a significant medical, psychological or medical issue; a bad school year with an unpleasant teacher; depression; anxiety; or other underlying emotional disorders.

As a result of trauma, some prevalent negative self-beliefs held by children are:

"I'm not safe."	"I'm weird (don't belong)"
"I'm bad."	"Bad things are going to happen."
"I'm not important."	"I can't ask for help."
"I am not heard by others."	"I can't ever be happy."
"I can't do anything right."	"I can't trust myself."
"I'm not good enough."	"I can't let my feelings out."

Because of these negative self-beliefs, children are often an easy target for spiritual warfare and the evil strategies of Satan.

As you begin the study, your child may or may not have expressed their hurts in life. You can begin to acknowledge and identify their hurts in their Timeline. Ask your child questions to help them identify their hurts and negative self beliefs. Some appropriate questions may be:

- "Remember the time when _____, how did that make you feel?"
- "When ____ happened, did you feel alone, overwhelmed, or hurt in your heart?"
- "Would you like to tell me what it was like for you when _____ happened?"
- "When ____ happened, did it make you think mean or bad things about yourself?"
- "I remember when ____ happened, you said (insert your child's voiced negative belief here)."
- "Have you had other times when you have thought (insert negative belief here)?"

What Is Spiritual Warfare?

Satan is the "god of this world," and he is the father of lies and deception. When an individual becomes a Christian and receives The Holy Spirit, they become part of God's family as well as part of the battle between good and evil.

The wicked one does not speak the truth, and *"When he lies, he speaks his native language, for he is a liar and the father of lies."* (John 8:44) Satan has a variety of methods, including quietly placing lies in our head. Through these thoughts, he encourages us to sin, and he masterfully tricks us with beliefs of self-doubt, guilt, and blame. In order to prepare your child for spiritual battle, he or she must recognize Satan's tactics and know how to fight back in a mighty way!

The Bible Study

The six week study can be done in various settings: within a family, in a youth group, or in a small group Bible study. Depending on the child and his or her reading level, there are from three to five days of work in each week.

For those in a group setting, please review group rules (Appendix C) with the participants at the start of each group. In the group, leaders can choose activities for the participants to share with one another. As an example, in week one they can present their *Timeline*, information about their family, or recite the week's memory verse. In subsequent weeks, leaders/parents can encourage participants to discuss the *Talk Together* questions, recite their memory verses, or read their statements from *The Truth* aloud. Parents may choose to discuss all or a few of the *Talk Together* questions; pick those that are relevant to your children and their identified hurts. Appendix B, at the back of the book, has a table of the weekly memory verses ready for your child to cut out and use as study cards.

In the Bible study, your child will begin by sharing information about themselves and their history. As the study progresses, he or she will learn the different aspects of spiritual warfare and how Satan negatively invades his or her thoughts and life. In the remaining weeks in the study, the children will learn how to protect themselves from Satan's destructive tactics.

The Bible study teaches your child to fight Satan with the truth about themselves, and with an understanding of how to use the full armor of God. The memory verses and *The Truth* section are valuable tools as they are part of your child's ammunition to fight the enemy. *The Truth* is an accurate, positive, and honest belief or statement about your child. The truth statements, along with memory verses, should be read aloud every day with the intent of memorization.

I pray you and your child find this study to be a time of connection between you, a time he or she grows closer to God, and lastly a time to learn how to fight against the enemy. My prayer is for your child to learn to fight like a mighty soldier of God!

Blessings,

Carol

Week One: My Story

Friends, let's begin the Bible study by getting to know one another. Please share the following information about yourself with the other group members.

My name is _____ and

I'm in the _____ grade.

My hobbies and interests are:

My favorite subject in school is:

Something most people don't know about me is:

In my free time, what I most enjoy doing is _____ and

what I like to do least is_____.

Memory Verse

You are altogether beautiful, my darling; there is no flaw in you.
Song of Solomon 4:7

More About The Memory Verse: My friend, you are a part of God's kingdom, one of His cherished children, and He is a part of you! Our Heavenly Father thinks you are an amazing kid . . . on the inside and out! And even when you sin or make a mistake, He thinks you are wonderful!

What are some things you like about yourself? (Write or draw your answer.)

Some of the things I love about myself and my family are: (Circle the ones that fit.)

They're fun	They love God	My mom is _____
My dad is ____	I have a dog	I have sister(s)
They're smart	I have a cat	I have brother(s)
I like school	I go to VBS	We like to play games

Other:

Other:

Other:

My Timeline

_____

Directions: On this timeline, mark and indicate significant events in your life. For example: your date of birth, hospitalizations, school changes, moves to a new community or home, sibling births, and any hurts you have experienced in life. (See an example timeline in Appendix A.)

THE TRUTH
1. I am an amazing kid!
2. God made me unique and special.
3. I love my family.

Talk Together

1. Introduce yourself to the others in your group. (If it's just you and your parent, practice introducing yourself to others!) Share your name, your grade, and where you go to school.

2. Show your timeline to the other participants. Point out and explain significant events in your life.

3. Apart from the group, identify with your parent or leader any event that has been hurtful in your life that continues to bother you, or has caused you to have negative or mean thoughts about yourself. Some examples can include: bullying, an unpleasant school year, family problems, multiple moves or moving to a new school or community, ongoing feelings of sadness or nervousness, or the unexpected loss of a loved one or beloved pet. You can share as much or as little as you like of your identified hurts with the group.

4. What do you hope to learn from the Bible study?

How Many Words Can You Make?
A CHILD OF THE KING

CROSS OUT

Directions: Cross Out any word that is a color, a number, has 2 Rs together or is a sport.

BORROW	JOY	SEVEN	YELLOW	SOCCER
CUTE	BARREL	RED	BALLET	PINK
LOVABLE	ONE	ORANGE	LACROSSE	TEN
BASEBALL	EIGHT	BLUE	ARROW	FUN
SPECIAL	TWO	WHITE	FURROW	SIX
THREE	PURPLE	DELIGHT	GOLF	GOLD
WORTHY	NINE	MARRY	SILVER	SORRY
FOUR	SPECIAL	HOCKEY	CARROT	SIX
BEAUTY	FOUR	TEAL	PARROT	FIVE

What do the words that are not crossed out have in common?

Week Two: God's Trustworthy Protection

Scripture: Psalm 33: 18-22

I Put My Trust In The Lord

18 But the Lord watches over those who fear him,
*   those who rely on his unfailing love.*
19 He rescues them from death
*   and keeps them alive in times of famine.*

20 We put our hope in the Lord.
*   He is our help and our shield.*
21 In him our hearts rejoice,
*   for we trust in his holy name.*
22 Let your unfailing love surround us, Lord,
*   for our hope is in you alone.*

Study The Scripture

As Christian believers, we are the children of God's kingdom; He watches over us, loves and adores us. In the Bible, one of the ways Christ shows His love for us is through the loving names he calls us: prince, princess, beloved, apple of His eye, His chosen, precious, My flock, and sons and daughters. The more we depend on God's love, the more we feel it and can begin to expect positive thoughts and love from others too.

Does God's names for you show you His love?

The Bible often mentions famine which is a shortage of food. Jeremiah 52: 6 says, *On the ninth day of the fourth month the famine was so severe in the city that there was no food for the people of the land.* A lack of food is a frightening, dangerous earthly problem because we need nutritious food for our bodies to grow and live. You may or may not have had a time of famine in your life but I want you to consider it . . . *Have you ever had a time of emotional famine? A time when you felt alone, scared, unloved, or unappreciated?*

Our Heavenly Father provides for us in miraculous ways even during a difficult or scary time. Father God faithfully watches over us, and He wants to protect us from everything and anyone. You may have had a time in your life when: other kids made fun of you or bullied you; when you had a family or medical problem; lost someone close to you; or you just kept feeling sad or nervous but weren't sure why you felt that way. During those times, it's normal for kids to feel alone, scared, or think no one cares about them. But even in those times, God is there watching over and helping His children.

Can you recall a time when God helped you?

Psalm 33, verse 22 says that The Lord's love is unfailing; we can depend on God. His love never fails us; He never gives up on us. (1 Corinthians 13:7) God always stands by us no matter what situation we are in or even when we mess us or make a poor decision . . . he continues to offer us His grace and forgiveness. At times, all children make mistakes, bad decisions, and sin. Children must learn from these situations to be able to grow into healthy adults. At the same time, a child must have an open heart and mind to learn how to make better choices.

We can *expect* good things from God. When we focus our hearts and eyes on the good things that God does for us, it helps us to experience more joy and contentment. Of course, the opposite is true too. When we focus on the negative in life, it makes us feel more depressed, downtrodden, hopeless, and unworthy.

How does your mind spend its time? On positive or negative thinking?

Memory Verse

What is the price of two sparrows—one copper coin? But not a single sparrow can fall to the ground without your Father knowing it. And the very hairs on your head are all numbered. So don't be afraid; you are more valuable to God than a whole flock of sparrows.

Matthew 10: 29-31

More About The Memory Verse: When Jesus was alive, sparrows were sold in the market as food for the poor; it was among the cheapest of foods. And just like all the birds you see in the sky, there were a lot of them. Our Father God loves every one of His sparrows; He *knows and cares* when even one of them falls to the ground! **If God loves each sparrow with a full heart, can you imagine how important you are to Him?** God tells us that He loves us so much, He counts every single hair on our head!

Bible Verse
*from the end of the earth I call to you
when my heart is faint.
Lead me to the rock
that is higher than I,*
Psalm 61:2

*But Jesus said, "Let the little children come to me. Don't stop them! For the Kingdom of
Heaven belongs to those who are like these children."*
Matthew 19:14

Define These Words

What do these words mean? Write a definition for the following words:

1. Unfailing-

2. Famine-

3. Faint-

4. Valuable-

Fill In The Blanks

from the end of the earth I call to you

   when my _____ is faint.

Lead me to the _____

   that is higher than I,

Psalm 61:2

But Jesus said, "Let the little children come to me. Don't stop them! For the Kingdom of _____ belongs to those who are like these _____."

Matthew 19:14

What is the price of two sparrows—one copper coin? But not a single sparrow can fall to the ground without your Father knowing it. And the very _____ on your head are all numbered. So don't be afraid; you are more _____ to God than a whole flock of sparrows.

Matthew 10: 29-31

THE TRUTH
Repeat these phrases out loud!

1. God loves me.
2. My Heavenly Father has always protected me.
3. God thinks I am: precious, beloved, chosen, and the apple of His eye.

Talk Together

1. Have you ever experienced something like an emotional famine? Have you ever had a time in your life when you felt alone, scared, unloved, or unappreciated?

2. How does your family show their love to you? Do you accept their comfort and affection or do you try to avoid or get away from it?

3. When you encounter a hurtful situation do you talk to your parents about it and let them help you? If you have kept these times to yourself, tell them about it now.

4. Share with the group some helpful strategies you use to keep your mind on positive thinking.

How Many Words Can You Make?
I CAN DEPEND ON GOD

Week Three: Satan is Sly

Scripture: Genesis 3:3-19

The Man and Woman Sin

3 The serpent was the shrewdest of all the wild animals the Lord God had made. One day he asked the woman, "Did God really say you must not eat the fruit from any of the trees in the garden?"

2 "Of course we may eat fruit from the trees in the garden," the woman replied. 3 "It's only the fruit from the tree in the middle of the garden that we are not allowed to eat. God said, 'You must not eat it or even touch it; if you do, you will die.'"

4 "You won't die!" the serpent replied to the woman. 5 "God knows that your eyes will be opened as soon as you eat it, and you will be like God, knowing both good and evil."

6 The woman was convinced. She saw that the tree was beautiful and its fruit looked delicious, and she wanted the wisdom it would give her. So she took some of the fruit and ate it. Then she gave some to her husband, who was with her, and he ate it, too. 7 At that moment their eyes were opened, and they suddenly felt shame at their nakedness. So they sewed fig leaves together to cover themselves.

8 When the cool evening breezes were blowing, the man and his wife heard the Lord God walking about in the garden. So they hid from the Lord God among the trees. 9 Then the Lord God called to the man, "Where are you?"

10 He replied, "I heard you walking in the garden, so I hid. I was afraid because I was naked."

11 "Who told you that you were naked?" the Lord God asked. "Have you eaten from the tree whose fruit I commanded you not to eat?"

12 The man replied, "It was the woman you gave me who gave me the fruit, and I ate it."

13 Then the Lord God asked the woman, "What have you done?"

"The serpent deceived me," she replied. "That's why I ate it."

14 Then the Lord God said to the serpent,

"Because you have done this, you are cursed
　more than all animals, domestic and wild.
You will crawl on your belly,
　groveling in the dust as long as you live.

15 And I will cause hostility between you and the woman,
   and between your offspring and her offspring.
He will strike your head,
   and you will strike his heel."

16 Then he said to the woman,

"I will sharpen the pain of your pregnancy,
   and in pain you will give birth.
And you will desire to control your husband,
   but he will rule over you."

17 And to the man he said,

"Since you listened to your wife and ate from the tree
   whose fruit I commanded you not to eat,
the ground is cursed because of you.
   All your life you will struggle to scratch a living from it.
18 It will grow thorns and thistles for you,
   though you will eat of its grains.
19 By the sweat of your brow
   will you have food to eat
until you return to the ground
   from which you were made.
For you were made from dust,
   and to dust you will return."

Bible Verse
Now the serpent was more crafty than any of the wild animals the Lord God had made. He said to the woman, "Did God really say, 'You must not eat from any tree in the garden'?
Genesis 3:1 NIV

Study The Scripture

In Genesis chapter 3, verse 3 how does God refer to the serpent? He calls the serpent, "shrewd." In the The New International Version (NIV) of the Bible, God calls the serpent, "crafty." The dictionary defines crafty as, "Skillful in underhand or evil schemes; cunning; deceitful; sly."

Satan disguises himself as a serpent. Needless to say, the serpent is sneaky and mean; he is unfair and does not care about the feelings of others!

At one time, Satan was one of God's beautiful angels but he became proud, jealous, full of hate. He wanted to be as an equal and as great as God. As a consequence, Satan was kicked out of heaven because he refused to obey God and he believed, *I will climb to the highest heavens and be like the Most High.* (Isaiah 14:14)

Satan wanted to turn Adam and Eve away from God; he used a charming voice to convince Eve to eat the fruit from the tree in the middle of the garden. Satan told her that if she ate the fruit she would be more like God. Of course, that was not possible! Eve also gave some of the fruit to Adam, and he ate it too.

All at once, they realized they had done something wrong! Adam and Eve had disobeyed God, and they became unhappy and fearful of Him. Before long, God came walking through the Garden, and Adam and Eve hid in the trees. When God asked them if they had eaten from the tree of knowledge, they avoided taking responsibility for their wrongdoing, and they placed blame on each other and on the serpent.

God was angry and sad about their choice, so He punished Adam, Eve, and the serpent. He gave them consequences that would be ours forever, and sent them out of the Garden.

God wants you to obey Him . . . not because He is mean or bossy, but because He loves you and wants you to be happy, safe, and protected! He wants you to obey your parents too.

Do you take responsibility for your choices? Whether they are good or bad?

Define These Words

1. Deceive-

2. Sly-

3. Cunning-

4. Manipulate-

> **Memory Verse**
>
> *Children are a gift from the Lord;
> they are a reward from him.*
> **Psalm 127:3**

More About The Memory Verse: Psalm 127, verse 3 tells us that all children are a precious gift from God. And you, my friend, are one of those gifts! God rewards His believers with children because they are the best reward in life . . . better than any house, jewel, or amount of money!

Do you believe you are a gift?

Fill In The Blanks

Now the serpent was more _____ than any of the wild animals the Lord God had made. He said to the woman, "Did God really say, 'You must not eat from any tree in the garden'?"

Genesis 3:1 NIV

Then the Lord God asked the woman, "What have you done?"

"The serpent _____ me," she replied. "That's why I ate it."

Genesis 3:13

Children are a _____ from the Lord; they are a _____ from him.

Psalm 127:3

The Truth
Remember: Repeat the truth out loud!

1. I am a gift from our Heavenly Father!
2. I am a reward to my mom and dad!

Talk Together

1. In Genesis, the serpent shows us he can be dishonest and sneaky. How does he manipulate and lie to Eve to convince her to eat the forbidden fruit?

2. Do you think there are times Satan whispers negative thoughts in your head, and tries to manipulate you? Identify and talk about some of those times.

3. What are some of the lies Satan tells you about yourself, your friends, or your family?

4. When God was walking in the Garden, He asked Adam and Eve, *"Have you eaten from the tree that I commanded you not to eat from?"* Circle Adam and Eve's answers. Did they take responsibility for their choices? Do you take responsibility for your good and bad choices? Or do you overly focus on your mistakes?

How Many Words Can You Make Out Of:
THE CRAFTY SERPENT

Week Four: Satan's Lies

Scripture: Matthew 4: 1-11

The Temptation of Jesus

Then Jesus was led by the Spirit into the wilderness to be tempted there by the devil. 2 For forty days and forty nights he fasted and became very hungry.

3 During that time the devil came and said to him, "If you are the Son of God, tell these stones to become loaves of bread."

4 But Jesus told him, "No! The Scriptures say,

*'People do not live by bread alone,
    but by every word that comes from the mouth of God.'"*

5 Then the devil took him to the holy city, Jerusalem, to the highest point of the Temple, 6 and said, "If you are the Son of God, jump off! For the Scriptures say,

*'He will order his angels to protect you.
And they will hold you up with their hands
    so you won't even hurt your foot on a stone.'"*

7 Jesus responded, "The Scriptures also say, 'You must not test the Lord your God.'"

8 Next the devil took him to the peak of a very high mountain and showed him all the kingdoms of the world and their glory. 9 "I will give it all to you," he said, "if you will kneel down and worship me."

10 "Get out of here, Satan," Jesus told him. "For the Scriptures say,

*'You must worship the Lord your God
    and serve only him.'"*

11 Then the devil went away, and angels came and took care of Jesus.

Study The Scripture

All Christians are part of a spiritual war between right (God) and wrong (Satan). The Bible tells us the enemy, Satan, is devious! He wants to turn your heart away from God and all that is good.

Satan's plans of attack are opposite to God's plans for us. Let's look at some examples of this: Satan's tactic is to lie, God's plan is truth; Satan wants to promote fear, God wants you to feel His love; Satan tries to discourage you, God wants you to feel courageous and strong; Satan wants you to do things "my way" whereas God wants you to do things His way; and finally, Satan wants to you be rude and angry, but God wants you to be patient and thoughtful.

In addition, Satan will lie and cheat to convince you that his evil beliefs are true. Satan uses three weapons to catch us off guard: lying, encouraging us to sin, and feelings of guilt or blame about our past sins or mistakes. Let's examine each of Satan's weapons more closely:

1. <u>Lies</u>-- Without even noticing, Satan whispers lies to you and makes you believe that his thoughts are your own . . . but they are not! His goal is to make you believe negative or bad things about yourself and others that are not true. Sometimes, Satan whispers so quietly that you believe his lies are your own thoughts, and that feels confusing.

2. <u>Encouragement to sin</u>-- Satan likes to tell you that poor choices are good and will not lead to trouble, but they always do! Satan encourages Jesus to sin when he says, *All this I will give you, if you will bow down and worship me.* Satan urges you to sin too. He'll try to convince you to keep your thoughts a secret and not talk about them with your parent or other trusted adult.

3. <u>Feelings of guilt or blame</u>-- Satan enjoys reminding believers of their past sin or embarrassing mistakes. You may notice thoughts of, *I'm so stupid* or *I always get in trouble!* Those mean thoughts about your sins or mistakes are Satan's way of rubbing the past in your face, but don't let him to do that to you!

In Matthew 4, Satan encourages Christ to sin when He is unprotected, in the wilderness, alone, and hungry. Satan loves to tempt us when we are by ourselves and exhausted. *Do you see how Satan tries to take advantage of us when we are defenseless?*

Satan wants you to doubt yourself, and he uses "If . . . " statements to cause doubt just like the ones he proposes to Jesus. *In Matthew 4:1-11, circle the "If . . . " statements spoken by Satan. How many do you find?*

Satan Tries to Bully Jesus
Satan aggravates Jesus, and says, "If You are the Son of God, command that these stones become bread." (4:3) Even though Christ was alone in the wilderness and worn down by hunger, He fights back. Jesus stands strong, relies on the word of God, leans on Him and answers, "Man shall not live on bread alone, but on every word that proceeds out of the mouth of God." (4:4)

Do you stand strong during doubt filled or hard times in your life?

For a second time, Satan teases Christ and says, "If you are the son of God . . . "(4:6) as he challenges Jesus to perform a miracle in front of Jerusalem. But Jesus does not fall for his evil trick and answers, "Do not put the Lord your God to the test." (4:7) In other words: Satan, do not bother me!

Do you tell Satan not to bother you?

Satan wants to trick us!
Satan will try the same tricks on you! He will lie, encourage you to sin, and make you think you're a bad kid with his tools of guilt and blame. He will lie and whisper that you are not one of God's precious children, even though you are!

And don't forget, Satan does this with sneaky questions and comments that he's designed to make you doubt yourself, your family, and God.

Some of Satan's tricky questions or comments in your head might be:
"Why can't I be happy?"
"Why can't I be like everyone else?"
"Why do bad things happen to me?"
"I'm stupid."
"God can't help me."
"Everything's always my fault."

Even though Satan has many tricks, remember that God knows all of them, and He is more powerful than Satan! Besides, once we are one of God's children, Satan can not have us but he sure can frustrate us!

Dig Deeper

Truth and goodness come from the Lord; lies and trickery come from Satan. So, if you're thinking something negative about yourself, your family, or God it's one of Satan's wicked lies. The most confusing part of Satan's lies is that they sound like your own voice, but in reality, it is his thoughts in your head.

What are some of the lies Satan wants you to believe about yourself and others? Look at the following list of lies, and circle any that you have crossed your mind. Afterward, look at the list of truths and circle those you believe are true about yourself and others. Add any additional ones to the lists.

LIES	TRUTH
I'm a bad kid	I'm a good kid
I'm stupid	I'm smart
God hates me	God loves me
I do not belong to God	I am one of God's children
There's something wrong with me	I'm fine as I am
I can't ever be happy	I can be happy
I can't ask for help	I can ask for help
I can't let my feelings out	It's safe to let my feelings out

Bad things are going to happen to me	It's safe now
It's my fault	It's not my fault
I should have done something	I did my best
I'm weak	I'm strong

Are you ready to battle the lies and embrace the truth? Begin by writing your own truths in *The Truth* section below. Remember, *The Truth* is to be repeated out loud everyday!

The Truth
Choose three truths about yourself from the list above.

1.

2.

3.

Bible Verse
The Lord himself watches over you!
The Lord stands beside you as your protective shade.
Psalm 121:5

So humble yourselves before God. Resist the devil, and he will flee from you.
James 4:7

Define These Words

1. Tempt--

2. Unprotected--

3. Exhausted--

4. Secure--

> **Memory Verse**
>
> *Keep me as the apple of your eye;*
> *hide me in the shadow of your wings*
> **Psalm 17:8**

More About The Memory Verse: My friend, God considers you to be a sweet and lovable child. He adores you!

The "apple" is the middle part, or pupil, in our eye. God created our face so that the pupils would be protected as they're the most sensitive part of our entire body. Just think about how much it hurts when your eye gets scratched or injured in any way. God tenderly considers and cares for every part of you!

God wants to protect you, and keep you safe just like a mother bird who keeps her little ones safe under her powerful, secure wings.

Fill In The Blanks

But Jesus told him, "No! The Scriptures say,

'People do not live by bread alone,

but by every _____ that comes from the _____ of God.'"

Matthew 4:4

Jesus responded, "The Scriptures also say, 'You must not _____ the Lord your God.'"

Matthew 4:7

Keep me as the _____ of your eye;

hide me in the shadow of your _____

Psalm 17:8

Talk Together

1. What are Satan's three favorite weapons to make you believe his lies?

2. Three times Satan uses *If . . .* statements to tempt Jesus to doubt Himself and The Father. How does Jesus fight back?

3. How can you tell the difference between your thoughts and Satan's? (Hint: Truth and goodness come from the Lord, and lies and trickery come from the evil one.)

4. If you're comfortable, share with the group the lies Satan tells you about yourself and your family. (If you're not comfortable, share the lie that Satan has cleverly placed in your thoughts.)

TEXT TWIST
(Make as many words as you can out of the following letters!)

F A T H E R G O D

Week Five: Fight Back!

Scripture: Ephesians 6:10-18

The Whole Armor of God

10 A final word: Be strong in the Lord and in his mighty power. 11 Put on all of God's armor so that you will be able to stand firm against all strategies of the devil. 12 For we are not fighting against flesh-and-blood enemies, but against evil rulers and authorities of the unseen world, against mighty powers in this dark world, and against evil spirits in the heavenly places.

13 Therefore, put on every piece of God's armor so you will be able to resist the enemy in the time of evil. Then after the battle you will still be standing firm. 14 Stand your ground, putting on the belt of truth and the body armor of God's righteousness. 15 For shoes, put on the peace that comes from the Good News so that you will be fully prepared. 16 In addition to all of these, hold up the shield of faith to stop the fiery arrows of the devil. 17 Put on salvation as your helmet, and take the sword of the Spirit, which is the word of God.

18 Pray in the Spirit at all times and on every occasion. Stay alert and be persistent in your prayers for all believers everywhere.

Study The Scripture

The Battle of Good versus Evil
The enemy, Satan, wants to keep us away from goodness, God, and heaven. Under these circumstances, we have to be prepared to fight the battle of good versus evil, and the only way we can win is with Christ by our side. We must always rely on Him and His power.

We have been given the whole armor of God[12] to stand our ground to Satan's schemes and spiritual attacks. The armor is our weapon to fight against Satan's plots; it brings us spiritual strength and courage to endure each battle and to fight for what is right and good. We must put on the armor, keep it on, and rely on it in every situation.

Here is a list of the full armor of God:

1. *SHIELD OF FAITH-* Our faith in Jesus is a shield, and protects our whole body from the fiery darts of Satan.

2. *HELMET OF SALVATION-* The helmet helps to guard our mind and thoughts from evil, stay focused on things that our good, and be continually thankful to the Lord.

---

[1] http://children.cccm.com/NTTeacherGuidePDF/CURNT332.pdf
[2] http://calvarystp.org/cm/devotionals/DEVNT332.pdf

3. *THE BREASTPLATE OF RIGHTEOUSNESS-* The breastplate protects our heart from Satan's tactics of lies, accusations, and reminders of past mistakes. Further, we protect our heart when we chose to do what God says is right.

4. *THE BELT OF TRUTH-* We protect our hearts and minds when we tell the truth, and bring God's truth into our lives by learning as much as possible about His ways.

5. *THE SWORD OF THE SPIRIT-* The Word of God, given to us by God and within us through the Holy Spirit, fights all the enemy's weapons.

6. *SHOES OF PEACE-* The shoes help us to claim the true peace that can only come from knowing the good news of Christ Jesus.

Lastly, we also rely on prayer to help us against Satan's tricks even though it is not a part of the whole armor of God.

Remember, you don't have to be afraid of this battle. God will help you stand against Satan and his darkness as He gives us the weapons and armor we need to stand strong.

Bible Verse

For the Spirit God gave us does not make us timid, but gives us power, love and self-discipline.
2 Timothy 1:7

I have given you authority to trample on snakes and scorpions and to overcome all the power of the enemy; nothing will harm you.
Luke 10:19

> **Memory Verse**
>
> *Jesus turned to Peter and said, "Get away from me, Satan! You are a dangerous trap to me. You are seeing things merely from a human point of view, not from God's."*
> **Matthew 16:23**

More About The Memory Verse: In Matthew 16:23, Jesus fearlessly tells Satan to get out of His way. Satan wants Jesus, and us, to stumble and fail. He wants us to sin, and tries to keep us from goodness and the purposes of God.

Does Satan get in your way of being a godly kid? A godly kid uses the whole armor of God and is honest, offers grace, helpful to others, and respects and obeys God and his or her parents.

The Truth
(Remember to repeat these out loud!)
1. God protects me!
2. I am a powerful warrior protected by the full armor of God.
3. I stand strong with God's word.

Define These Words

1. Armor--

2. Righteousness--

3. Fearless--

4. Mighty--

Fill In The Blanks

A final word: Be _____ in the Lord and in his _____ power.

Ephesians 6:10

Jesus turned to Peter and said, "Get away from me, Satan! You are a _____ trap to me. You are seeing things merely from a _____ point of view, not from God's."

Matthew 16:23

For the Spirit God gave us does not make us timid, but gives us _____, _____ and _____-_____.

2 Timothy 1:7

Talk Together

1. Does Satan "go easy" on kids? Does he leave them alone?

2. Name and describe all six of the items in the full armor of God:

3. How can you use the whole armor of God in your battle against Satan's lies?

4. What is another helpful tool we mentioned to battle Satan that's not included in the armor of God?

5. Write a prayer asking God to protect you from Satan's evil schemes in your life:

How Many Words Can You Make Out of:
BELT OF TRUTH

Put On Your Armor!
Draw a picture of yourself wearing the Whole Armor of God.

Week Six: God is My Helper, My Protector

Scripture: Psalm 121: 1-8

My Help Comes From the Lord

1 I look up to the mountains—
does my help come from there?

2 My help comes from the Lord,
who made heaven and earth!

3 He will not let you stumble;
the one who watches over you will not slumber.

4 Indeed, he who watches over Israel
never slumbers or sleeps.

5 The Lord himself watches over you!
The Lord stands beside you as your protective shade.

6 The sun will not harm you by day,
nor the moon at night.

7 The Lord keeps you from all harm
and watches over your life.

8 The Lord keeps watch over you as you come and go,
both now and forever.

Study The Scripture

The Lord - My Helper, My Protector

When we run into troubles, the hardship can feel bigger, taller, and wider than any mountain. On our own, we cannot triumph over those large and looming problems, but with the Lord by our side, we always overcome. God faithfully promises to be there, to catch us when we fall, and to be our comfort and protection along the way.

Under the protective shade of the Lord, we are kept out of harm's way by day and by night. He constantly watches over us, and He never takes a break. God promises to "never leave you or forsake you" (Hebrews 13:5), and He never fails in any of His promises to us.

There probably have been times in the past where you faced problems . . . big or small. You might have had times when you felt lost, alone, abandoned, or afraid. You may have: lost a parent, been bullied at school, had medical issues or disabilities, been left out, lost a home or had to move, had an upsetting situation with a sibling, or had a friend who turned their back on you time and time again.

For those who love and serve God, He promises that every detail of our life is made into something good. (Romans 8:28) *Every detail . . .* that includes the things in your past that were hard, scary, or just plain bad.

What are the details that you thought were too bad --even for God?

Well, guess what? Nothing is too hard for God. He knows every single thing that happened to you, and He hated it! He cried in anguish about that things that were happening to you! **And even if you didn't know Him then, He never left your side. He never left you alone.**

Looking back, how do you know God was there with you?

Even if you didn't know God then, you have come to know Him now. God and the angels in Heaven rejoice that you know Him. Most of all, God loves to hear you say the truth --you are one of His precious children! And this was God's plan for you, *They are plans for good and not for disaster, to give you a future and a hope.* (Jeremiah 29:11)

Bible Verse

For the Lord your God is living among you.
He is a mighty savior.
He will take delight in you with gladness.
With his love, he will calm all your fears.
He will rejoice over you with joyful songs."
Zephaniah 3:17

3 All praise to God, the Father of our Lord Jesus Christ. God is our merciful Father and the source of all comfort. 4 He comforts us in all our troubles so that we can comfort others. When they are troubled, we will be able to give them the same comfort God has given us.
2 Corinthians 1:3-4

Define These Words

1. Slumber-

2. Looming-

3. Triumph-

4. Hardship-

> **Memory Verse**
>
> Give thanks to the Lord, for he is good!
> His faithful love endures forever.
> **1 Chronicles 16:34**

More About The Memory Verse: My friend, I know you have experienced some hard times in your life whether they have been big or small. So, any time your brain has negative thoughts (for example, "I'm a bad kid" or "Bad things happen to me") you may feel a hurt or anger in your heart. That's because your brain is connecting back to your past hurts.

You may even have worries that these things will happen again in the future. It's okay that you have this worry, but know that over time and through resolution it will get better!

For those of us with worries, it's comforting to know that our faithful God will always stand beside us like a mighty warrior. (Jeremiah 20:11) He is always right beside you, holding your precious hand with His, and covering you with His fluffy wings of eternal comfort.

The Truth

1. God is always by my side; He will never leave me.
2. My Heavenly Father makes something good out of every situation in my life.
3. God wants to give me hope and a bright future.

Fill In The Blanks

Give thanks to the Lord, for he is _____!

His faithful love endures _____.

1 Chronicles 16:34

All praise to God, the Father of our Lord Jesus Christ. God is our merciful Father and the source of all _____. He comforts us in all our troubles so that we can comfort others. When they are troubled, we will be able to give them the same _____ God has given us.

2 Corinthians 1:3-4

And we know that God causes _____ to work together for the _____ of those who love God and are called according to his purpose for them.

Romans 8:28

Talk Together

1. Share with the group any life troubles that you have not mentioned in past weeks. Especially ones that you thought were "too small" or "too bad" . . . Remember: there aren't any problems that are too small or bad for God; they are all important to Him.

2. Looking back, how do you know God never left your side in every situation?

3. What are some of the good things that have come out of your past hard times?

4. How surprising is it that God can make good things even out of a bad situation?

Text Twister
(Use these letters to make as many words as you can!)

H A R D S H I P

Appendix A

Timeline Example:

This is an example timeline for 10 year old, Sophie. Notice the significant dates and events in her life are listed on the timeline. The timeline is a visual aid for the parent and child, allowing you both to see what large T and small t events the child has experienced in life.

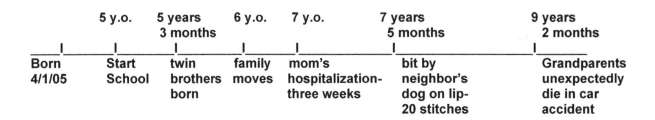

Appendix B

MEMORY VERSE STUDY CARDS

You are altogether beautiful, my darling; there is no flaw in you. **Song of Solomon 4:7**	*What is the price of two sparrows—one copper coin? But not a single sparrow can fall to the ground without your Father knowing it. And the very hairs on your head are all numbered. So don't be afraid; you are more valuable to God than a whole flock of sparrows.* **Matthew 10: 29-31**	*Children are a gift from the Lord; they are a reward from him.* **Psalm 127:3**
Keep me as the apple of your eye; hide me in the shadow of your wings **Psalm 17:8**	*Jesus turned to Peter and said, "Get away from me, Satan! You are a dangerous trap to me. You are seeing things merely from a human point of view, not from God's."* **Matthew 16:23**	*Give thanks to the Lord, for he is good! His faithful love endures forever.* **1 Chronicles 16:34**

Appendix C

GROUP RULES

1. Give your full attention to the group.

2. What is shared in the group, stays in the group- Confidentiality.

3. One person talks at a time.

4. You can pass if you don't want to share.

5. Be honest and respectful to everyone.

6. Have fun!

Made in the USA
Las Vegas, NV
30 June 2023

74093991R00031